T0198831

AN OKIE'S
OUTSIDE LOOK
—— INSIDE ——
BASEBALL

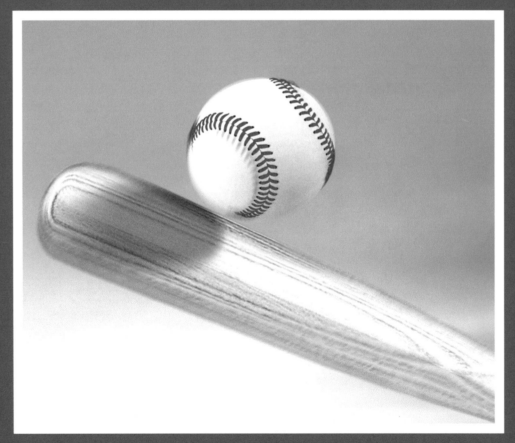

L CHADWICK BOWMAN

© 2020 L Chadwick Bowman. All rights reserved.

No part of this book may be reproduced, stored in a retrieval system, or transmitted by any means without the written permission of the author.

AuthorHouse™
1663 Liberty Drive
Bloomington, IN 47403
www.authorhouse.com
Phone: 1 (800) 839-8640

Because of the dynamic nature of the Internet, any web addresses or links contained in this book may have changed since publication and may no longer be valid. The views expressed in this work are solely those of the author and do not necessarily reflect the views of the publisher, and the publisher hereby disclaims any responsibility for them. This book is printed on acid-free paper.

Any people depicted in stock imagery provided by Getty Images are models, and such images are being used for illustrative purposes only. Certain stock imagery © Getty Images.

Print information available on the last page.

ISBN: 978-1-7283-4410-2 (sc)
ISBN: 978-1-7283-4409-6 (hc)
ISBN: 978-1-7283-4411-9 (e)

Published by AuthorHouse 01/20/2020

authorHOUSE®

Why another book about baseball?

I grew up in a little place in south central Oklahoma where you spent summer playing baseball in the local church leagues. My brothers and I played for Bray Missionary Baptist Church at Bray. That was long before Little League took over. We played in the Marlow Church League. I mention this because this is where I got the love for baseball. My father was a baseball fan and taught all his kids, girls too, about the game.

In school at Bray Public School you played baseball and basketball, if you were a boy, girls just had basketball. I came from a family of 10 children, 4 girls and 6 boys. Nine of the ten grew to adulthood. There was 23 years difference from the first child to the last. Exactly 23 years. I was born on my oldest sister's 23rd birthday. Lucky girl. The reason I mentioned her was because she had a step-son a two years older than me, Louis Halford that I played baseball with every summer and we both collected baseball cards. When we couldn't play ball we played games with our cards.

From this came my love for more than playing the game. I loved statistics, reading where the players were from, how many were all-stars, or played in the World Series. I would listen to the Cardinals or Astros on the radio at night (it was tough when they were on the west coast). I remember taking the radio, after asking permission, to school so we could listen to the World Series. Remember, night games didn't start in the Series until 1971.

I recall the 1967 series between the Red Sox and Cardinals. I was a Cardinal fan, Bob Gibson, Lou Brock, Tim McCarver, and the rest was my team. I also liked the Red Sox though. Yazstrzemski, Petrocelli, Aparacio, Howard, and the rest. Gibby won 3 games and Brock stole 7 bases as the Cards won in seven games. A classic. In 1968 the Cards played the Tigars. In game one, Gibby broke Sandy Koufax's strikeout record for a single game and Brock stole seven more bases in the series. Kaline, Northrup, Freehan, McLain, Lolich, and the other Tigars would win in seven games. Lolich would outduel Gibson in game seven for the win.

It was this love for baseball that I decided to write this book. Things I learned, remembered, saw, heard, and read. I want to share with other baseball fans and drive an interest to those who don't share my love for the game. My dream was to one day play in the majors, but I accepted that I wasn't good enough. I aslo wanted to be an announcer and sports reporter. I finally got to be a reporter at Konawa, Oklahoma for their football and basketball teams. Coleman, Oklahoma baseball and basketball too.

I would do anything to be a part of baseball. I coached little league in Duncan, Oklahoma, Coleman, Oklahoma, and Caddo, Oklahoma. I worked as an umpire for little league baseball and softball in Bray. Then I umpired high school for five years, but heart problems forced me to give that up.

Then I started coaching softball, slow pitch and fast, for several years. It was fun, but not baseball. I enjoyed coaching in all phases though. I was an excitable coach, to say the least. I once threatened to use a bat on a punk for running over my catcher, a 15-year-old girl. I was never thrown out of a game, but came close. As an ump, I tossed only on person, a coach, from Konawa.

This book is all mine. I put what I want in here and only what I want in here. You will not find any praise or worship of Ty Cobb or Cap Anson. Both hall-of-famers, but they were racist, bigots, and dirty players. Cobb once said he didn't like niggers, Jews, wops, dagos, spics, or Indians.

Anson took his team to play once and the opposing team had a black catcher, Moses Fleetwood, and Anson told the opposing team if the nigger plays we won't. Commissioner Kenesaw Landis was also a raciest. Now I've got a problem with the fact that these men are still in the Hall. Pete Rose can't be inducted because he bet on his team. So did Cobb, but being a friend of Commish Landis bailed him out. Barry Bonds, Mark McGuire, Roger Clemens, Sammy Sosa and other are not getting votes because they used PERFORMANCE ENHANCING DRUGS (PEDs).

Baseball was losing its fans, popularity, after going on strike, but a homerun race changed all that. When McGwire, Sosa, and Ken Griffey Jr started a race for 61, all of America tuned in. Especially when it turned to a two-man race, Big Mac and Slammin' Sammy. What a race. Then along came Bonds to shatter McGuire's record.

I understand that PEDs may let a man hit the ball harder and throw it harder, but it don't give them eyes to see or quickness to swing nor control to throw. I was once an opponent to these guys, but now I say "Let them in". Rose is the greatest hitter of all-time, Bonds the greatest long ball hitter, Clemens one of the greatest strikeout pitchers. If we can allow raciest bigots in the Hall then let these guys in too. Or take out the haters. You would be surprised how small the Hall would become.

If I could time travel I would go back and watch these sport stars: (1) Jim Thorpe, playing ANYTHING, (2) Satchel Paige in his prime, (3) Chief Bender, (4) Jim Brown not only a football star, but lacrosse too, (5) Pete Maravich, (6) Honus Wagner, (7) Jackie Robinson playing ANYTHING, (8) Jesse Owens, (9) Negro League Baseball, (10) Women's Baseball League, (11) Babe Didrickson play ANYTHING, (12) Jim Shoulders, (13) Cool Papa Bell, (14) Yogi Berra, (15) Christy Mathewson, (16) Nolan Ryan, (17) Bob Feller, (18) Larry Mahan, (19) Gail Sayers, (20) Barry Sanders, (21) Wilt Chamberlain, (22) Don Meredith, (23) Nadia Cominech, (24) Walter Johnson, and (25) Bob Ueker. Okay, that last one was a reach, but I'd love to sit by him for one game.

If you have a complaint about how I feel or what I write all I can say is, "Write your own." I just want people to enjoy this book and somewhere say "WOW, I didn't know that." Please

enjoy and share what you learn.

BASEBALL TEAMS:

BRAVES

1876 – 1882 Boston Red Caps

1883 – 1906 Boston Beaneaters

1907 – 1910 Boston Doves

1911 Boston Rustlers

1912 – 1935 Boston Braves

1936 – 1940 Boston Bees

1941 – 1952 Boston Braves

1953 -1965 Milwaukee Braves

1966 – Present Atlanta Braves

CUBS

1876 – 1889 White Stockings

1890 – 1892 Colts

1898 – 1901 Orphans

1902 – Present Cubs

BROWN Chicago Nat'l

PHILLIES

1880 – 1882 Worcester
          Brown Stockings
1890 – 1941 Philadelphia Phillies
1942 Phils, 1943 Phillies
1944 -1945 Blue Jays
1946 – Present Phillies

GIANTS

1883 – 1884 Gothams

1885 – 1957 New York Giants

1958 – Present San

Francisco Giants

CARDINALS

1884 – 1891 Browns (American Association)
1892 – 1898 Browns
1889 Perfectos
1900 – Present Cardinals

PIRATES

1887 – 1889 Alleghenies

1890 Innocents

1891 – Present Pirates

DODGERS

1890 – 1898 Bidegrooms

1899 – 1910 Superbas

1911 – 1913 Dodgers

1914 – 1931 Robins

1932 – 1957 Brooklyn Dodgers

1958 – Present Los Angeles
Dodgers

REDS

1890 – 1943 Reds

1944 – 1945 Red Legs

1946 – 1953 Reds

1954 – 1960 Redlegs

1961 – Present Reds

ATHLETICS

1901 – 1954 Philadelphia Athletics

1955 – 1961 Kansas City Athletics

1962 – 1967 A's,

1968 – 1986 Oakland A's

1987 – Present Athletics

INDIANS

1901 – 1902 Bluebirds (or Blues)

1903 – 1911 Naps (after
Napoleon Lajoia)

1912 – 1914 Molly McGuires

1915 – Present Indians

ORIOLES

1901 Milwaukee Brewers

1902 – 1953 St Louis Browns

1954 – Present Baltimore Orioles

RED SOX

1901 – 1907 Americans

1908 – Present Red Sox

YANKEES

1901 – 1902 Baltimore Orioles

1903 – 1912 New York
Highlanders

1913 – Present Yankees

WHITE SOX

1901 – 1902 White Stockings

1903 – Present White Sox

TIGERS

1901 – Present

SCHMIDT DETROIT

COBB DETROIT

TWINS

1901 – 1905 Washington Senators

1906 – 1956 Nationals

1957 – 1960 Senators

1961 – Present Minnesota Twins

ANGELS

1961 – 1964 Los Angeles Angels

1965 – 1996 California Angels

1992 – Present Anaheim Angels

ASTROS

1962 – 1964 Colt 45's / Colts

1965 – 1997 National
    League Astros

1998 – Present American
    League Astros

METS

1962 – Present

Printed in the United States
By Bookmasters